P9-DDV-122

VOTING IN ELECTIONS

by Amy Kortuem

PEBBLE
a capstone imprint

Pebble Explore is published by Pebble, an imprint of Capstone.
1710 Roe Crest Drive
North Mankato, Minnesota 56003
www.capstonepub.com

Library of Congress Cataloging-in-Publication Data is available on the Library of Congress website.
ISBN 978-1-9771-1400-6 (hardcover)
ISBN 978-1-9771-1824-0 (paperback)
ISBN 978-1-9771-1408-2 (ebook pdf)

Summary: Describes elections, who can vote, why voting is important, and more.

Photo Credits
Alamy: Peter Titmuss, 18, RBM Vintage Images, 14; iStockphoto: adamkaz, Cover; Library of Congress Prints and Photographs, 11, 12; NASA, 28; Newscom: Frances M. Roberts, 25, John Delapp/Design Pics, 9, Reuters/Joshua Roberts, 27, TNS/Al Diaz, 19; Shutterstock: Everett Historical, 13, Jeremy Bustin Photography, 16, Joseph Sohm, 6-7, 20, Lisa F. Young, 23, Maverick Pictures, 17, montira areepongthum, 5, Rob Crandall, 21, 22, Steve Heap, 26

Design Elements
Shutterstock: Anatolir, Nadezhda Molkentin

Editorial Credits
Anna Butzer, editor; Cynthia Della-Rovere, designer;
Jo Miller, media researcher; Laura Manthe, production specialist

All internet sites appearing in back matter were available and accurate when this book was sent to press.

Printed and bound in China.
2489

Table of Contents

Words in **bold** are in the glossary.

What Is Voting?

Let's say your town needs a new playground. But first the town needs to know how many people want a new playground. How does the town find out? They hold an **election**, and people **vote**!

Voting also happens in small ways. Families can vote on what to have for dessert. You and your friends can vote on which game to play during recess. Voting is a way to find out what most people want.

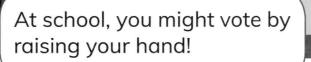

At school, you might vote by raising your hand!

The U.S. government is a **democracy**. People have the right to choose the country's leaders.

People vote for the person they feel will do the best job.

Voting gives people a voice in government. They vote for the leaders of their cities and states. They vote for the president to lead the United States.

Who Can Vote?

Voting is important! There are a few rules about who can do it. People must be at least 18 years old to vote. They also must be U.S. **citizens**.

In most states, citizens must **register** to vote. When there is an election, they can vote. No one can make a person vote. No one can stop others from voting. Citizens do not pay to vote.

People must register to vote before an election.

There was a time when not everyone could vote. In the early 1800s, only white men could vote. For years, other people worked hard to win voting **rights**. In 1870, African American men finally won the right to vote.

President Grant (center) signed the law giving black men the right to vote in 1870.

Women wanted to vote too. They gave speeches and wrote letters. They held marches and carried signs to **protest**. In 1920, women won the right to vote. Now women and men have the same voting rights.

Women marching in 1915

Women protesting in front
of the White House in 1918

Some states tried to make it hard for African Americans to vote. They wanted African Americans to pass tests and pay fees before they could vote.

In 1965, a law was passed that made these things illegal. People who do not read or speak English can vote because of this law too.

Who Do We Vote For?

People vote for the **candidate** they like best. A candidate is someone who wants to work for the government. A candidate might want to be the leader of a city or state. A candidate might want to be president and lead the United States.

Candidates have ideas about
how they will do the job. They make
promises about what they will do as
a leader. They talk about how they will
do this better than other candidates.

Candidates have **campaigns** to share their ideas. They talk to people about the things they will do if they win. They **advertise** on TV and the radio. They advertise on the internet and in newspapers too. They mail cards and letters printed with their campaign information.

During a debate, candidates talk about what they would do if elected.

Sometimes candidates have **debates** about their ideas. People can watch the debates on TV. Debates help people decide who they want to vote for.

How Do We Vote?

We vote in elections. Elections happen at certain times. We vote for members of **Congress** every two years. We vote for the U.S. president every four years.

During election years, Election Day is on a Tuesday at the beginning of November. Some people want to make Election Day a national holiday. This would make it easy for all people to vote.

On Election Day, people go to **polling places** to vote. Voters mark **ballots** with the candidates they like. Sometimes they mark paper ballots. Then they put the ballot into an electronic reader. Sometimes they vote on an electronic voting machine's screen.

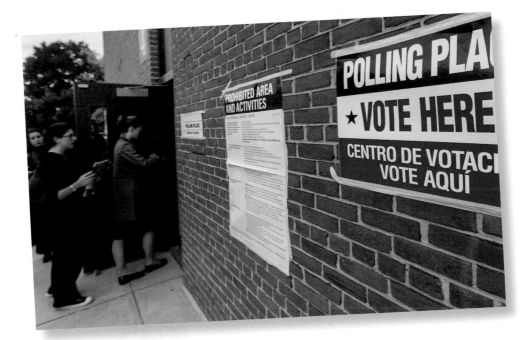

Some people use electronic machines to vote.

Why Do People Vote?

We vote for many reasons. When we vote, we choose people who make laws. The people we choose help lead our government. We pick the mayor we think will help our town the most. We choose the president we think will do the best job for our country.

Ballots include the names of the candidates in an election.

Many Americans chose not to vote. This means they do not help choose who works for our government. Some people think their votes don't matter. This is not true. Every vote makes a difference.

Voting is an American right. It is a **responsibility** of a good citizen. Voting doesn't just help ourselves. It helps the whole country.

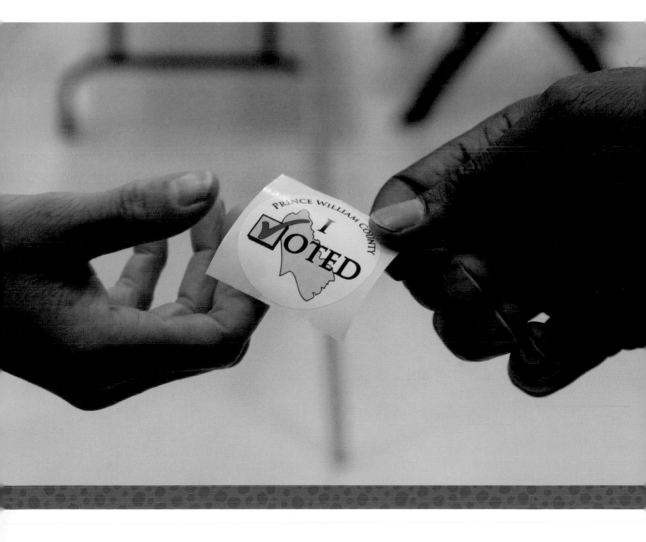

Did You Know?

Many polling places give out "I Voted" stickers. They hope other people see these stickers and will go vote.

American citizens living outside the United States can vote too. Even those who are very far away! Astronauts have voted from outer space in 1997 and in 2004.

Astronaut Shane Kimbrough voted from space in 2016.

Fast Facts

- American citizens can vote when they are at least 18 years old.

- African-American men gained the right to vote in 1870.

- Women could not vote until 1920.

- American citizens can vote if they are in another country—or even in space!

- It is against the law to stop someone else from voting.

- Election Day is always on a Tuesday in early November.

Glossary

advertise (AD-vuhr-tize)—to give information about something

ballot (BAL-uht)—a piece of paper, or a card, used to vote in an election

campaign (kam-PAYN)—a series of actions planned to bring about a specific result

candidate (KAN-di-date)—a person who runs for office, such as president

citizen (SIT-i-zuhn)—a member of a country; a person becomes a citizen at birth or when they choose to become one as an adult

Congress (KAHNG-gruhs)—the branch of the U.S. government that makes laws, consisting of the House of Representatives and the Senate

debate (di-BAYT)—a discussion between two sides with different ways of thinking on a subject; each side tries to convince people that it is right

democracy (di-MOK-ruh-see)—a kind of government in which the people make decisions by voting

election (i-LEK-shuhn)—the process of choosing someone or deciding something by voting

polling place (POHL-ing PLAYSS)—a place where people vote

protest (pro-TEST)—to object to something strongly and publicly

register (REJ-uh-stur)—to enter a voter's name on an official list

responsibility (ri-spon-suh-BIL-uh-tee)—a duty or job

rights (RITES)—things that everyone has a right to, such as the right to freedom and to not be treated unfairly

vote (VOHT)—choice made by a person based on their own views

Read More

Christelow, Eileen. *Vote!* Boston: Houghton Mifflin Harcourt, 2018.

Manning, Jack. *Voting in Elections.* North Mankato, MN: Capstone Press, 2015.

Shamir, Ruby. *What's the Big Deal About Elections?* New York: Philomel Books, 2018.

Internet Sites

Ducksters: How Voting Works
https://www.ducksters.com/history/us_government_voting.php

Kids Voting USA
https://kidsvotingusa.org/about-us

Index